USBORNE
SCIENCE ACTIVITIES

Helen Edom, Moira Butterfield,
Rebecca Heddle and Mike Unwin

Designed by Sandy Wegener, Susie McCaffrey,
Non Figg and Ian McNee

Illustrated by Kate Davies

Contents

SCIENCE WITH
AIR

Consultant: Geoffrey Puplett

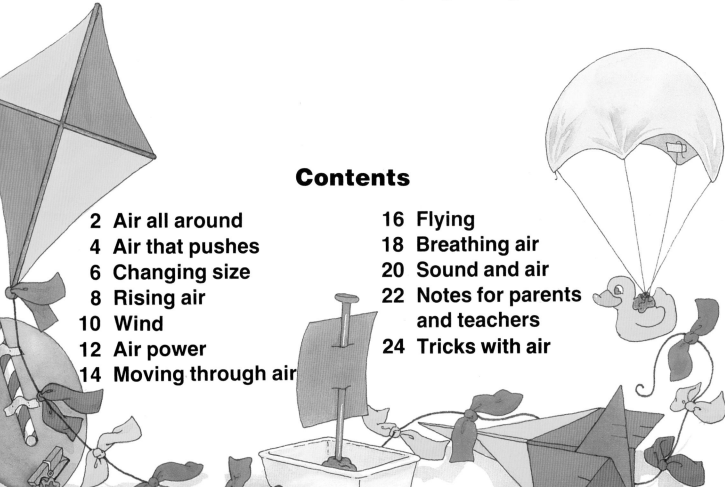

Contents

Air all around

Although you cannot see it, air is all around you. Try the experiments in this part of the book to find out some of the things that air can do.

Things you need

The things you need for the experiments are easy to find. Here are some to collect.

Plastic bottles

Cartons

Bowl

Balloons

Straws

Feeling air

How can you tell that air is all around you? Try flapping some cardboard next to your face.

The cardboard makes the air move. You can feel the air moving against your cheek.

Being a scientist

Before you do an experiment, guess what will happen. Watch to see if you are right and write down what you find out.

The atmosphere

All around the earth there is a thick blanket of air called the atmosphere. Outside in space, above the atmosphere, there is no air at all.

2

A paper race

Moving air can push things around. You can use it to make this game work.

You need a piece of cardboard and a strip of paper for each player. Fold up one end of each strip.

You could add faces.

Fold here.

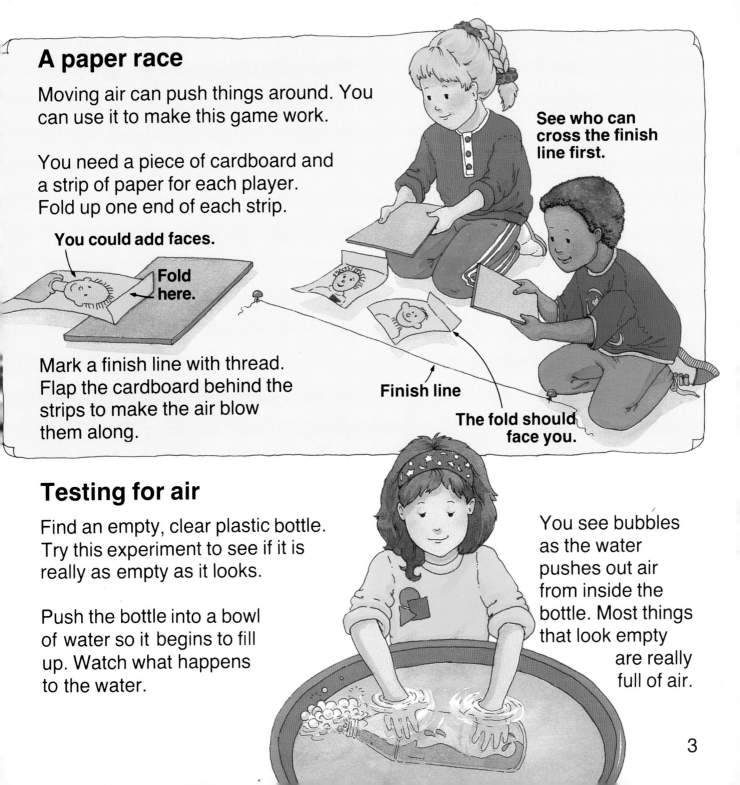

See who can cross the finish line first.

Mark a finish line with thread. Flap the cardboard behind the strips to make the air blow them along.

Finish line

The fold should face you.

Testing for air

Find an empty, clear plastic bottle. Try this experiment to see if it is really as empty as it looks.

Push the bottle into a bowl of water so it begins to fill up. Watch what happens to the water.

You see bubbles as the water pushes out air from inside the bottle. Most things that look empty are really full of air.

3

Air that pushes

Air pushes against things all the time. You are so used to it pushing against you that you do not notice it.

Heavy newspaper

Tear a sheet of newspaper in half and smooth it out on a table. Put a ruler under the paper so it sticks out over the edge of the table.

Use a new newspaper.

Stand to one side so the ruler cannot hit you.

Press down on the ruler to see if you can flick it off the table.

This is surprisingly hard to do because air presses down on the newspaper, keeping it in place.

4

Upside-down trick

This trick can be messy so try it over a bowl.

Fill a plastic cup full of water so the water bulges up above the top.

Put some cardboard on top and turn the cup upside-down, holding the cardboard in place.

Make sure there are no gaps between the cardboard and the cup.

Let go of the cardboard and see what happens.

Air pushes up on the cardboard and keeps it in place. This makes the water stay in the cup.

Collapsing carton

Sip all the drink out of a juice carton. Keep on sipping so you empty out the air. Watch what happens.

Use a cardboard carton with a hole for a straw.

When the carton is completely empty, the air outside pushes in the carton's sides.

Take the straw out of your mouth and watch the carton.

Air

The sides go out again because air rushes into the carton and pushes them out.

See what happens to the carton if you blow even more air into it.

Pumping up

Try pumping up a bicycle tire. Keep feeling the tire with your fingers to see how hard it is.

Air pushes harder when it is squeezed together. The more air you put inside the tire, the harder the tire feels.

Powerful tires

Air-filled tires are strong enough to take the weight of heavy trucks and tractors.

Changing size

When air gets warmer it expands, which means that it spreads out.

Disappearing dent

Watch what happens if you warm up the air inside a ping-pong ball.

Cover the glass, with a plate for example, to keep the ball down.

Watch the dent carefully.

First push a dent into the ball. Then put it in a glass full of warm water.

The water heats up the air in the ball, so the air expands. The expanding air pushes out the dent.

A jumping coin

You can use expanding air to make a coin jump.

Stand a long-necked bottle in a deep bowl. Wet the rim of the bottle and set a large coin on top. Then pour warm water into the bowl.

The coin must cover the hole completely.

The warm water heats up the air inside the bottle. The air spreads out and pushes the coin upward.

Hold the bottle to keep it from falling over.

Getting colder

Try this experiment to find out what happens when air becomes colder.

You could use an empty soda bottle.

First, put some ice-cubes into a plastic bag and crush them with a rolling pin. Then put the ice in a plastic bottle. Screw on the lid.

Shake the bottle, then put it down. Watch what happens to the bottle as the ice cools the air inside.

Thunderstorms

In thunderstorms, lightning heats the air around it. The air expands so quickly that it makes a loud noise. You hear this noise as thunder.

When air cools, it shrinks. The bottle's sides go inward so no empty space is left inside.

The cold air takes up less space.

7

Rising air

When air gets warmer it becomes lighter, so it moves upward.

Flying feather

Drop a small pillow feather above a warm radiator. See which way the feather floats.

Do not try this experiment above a fire.

The radiator heats up the air above it. The warm air rises and pushes up the feather.

Hot air balloons

Huge balloons can carry people underneath them. Burners heat the air in the balloon to make it rise. When the people want to land, they let the air cool again so the balloon sinks to the ground.

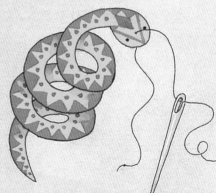

Wriggly snake

You can use warm air to make this snake wriggle.

Use a needle to push a thread through the snake's head.

Draw around a plate to make a circle on paper. Cut out the circle.

Draw around and around inside the circle to make a spiral. Color the spiral like a snake, then cut it out.

Flowing air

In cold weather, go into a room with its heating on and close the door.

Hold a strip of tissue by the bottom of the door. See if the tissue moves.

Watch the end of the tissue strip.

The air in the heated room rises as it warms up. Colder air flows under the door to fill the space left by the rising air. This cold flow of air makes the tissue flutter.

Hang or hold the snake above a radiator.

The rising air makes the snake move.

Why there is wind

Wind happens because the Sun warms up parts of the land and sea. These warm parts heat up the air above them, like a radiator.

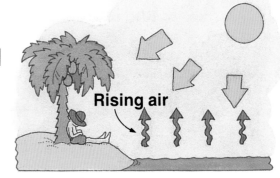

Rising air

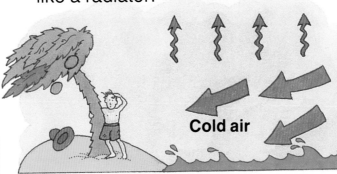

Cold air

The warm air rises and cold air flows into the space beneath. This flow of air is the wind.

9

Wind

The wind is moving air. You can feel it push against you and see it blowing things around.

Strong and gentle

Look out for things that move in the wind.

A gentle wind, called a breeze, can make smoke drift, flags flutter and leaves rustle.

A very strong wind, called a gale, can make whole trees sway and branches break.

Dangerous winds

The strongest winds of all are called hurricanes. Hurricanes can travel at 320 kilometres per hour (200 mph) and blow away trees and buildings.

Changing wind

See if you can tell which way the wind is blowing. These tests will help.

Wet your finger and hold it up. It feels coldest on the side the wind is coming from.

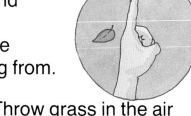

Throw grass in the air and watch which way the wind blows it.

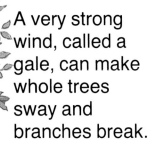

Try the tests at different times to see how often the wind changes direction.

Wind and rain

Look out for moving clouds in the sky. The wind moves clouds around from place to place, bringing the rain with them.

Make a weather vane

You can make a weather vane to help you find out where the wind comes from.

Mark the directions, north, south, east and west on cardboard (see below).

Early in the morning, go outside and place the card so east points toward the Sun.*** Now all the directions are in the right place.

In the early morning, the Sun is always in the east.

Cut an arrow out of cardboard. Tape it to the cotton reel. Glue a circle of cardboard on top.

Make the tail large like this.

Put a blob of model dough in the middle of the directions and push in the needle, point upward. Put the reel on top.

This arrow shows that the wind is coming from the north.

Use stones to keep the cardboard flat.

The arrow points in the direction the wind is coming from.

You could make a chart like this to show the direction and strength of the wind on different days.

Day	M	T	W
Direction	N		
Strength	weak		

Winds are named after the direction they blow from. For instance, a north wind blows from the north.

***Never look straight at the Sun as it can burn your eyes.

*Empty thread spool.   **Cellophane tape.

Air power

You can use air to make things move. Try these ideas, then see if you can find any more ways to use air power.

Sailing boats

Float an empty plastic tub in some water. Try to blow it along.

Now push a knitting needle through some paper to make a sail. Use model dough to stand the needle up in the tub.

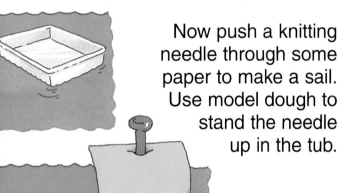

See how easily you can blow the boat along now.

More air can push against the sail so the boat moves faster. Try different-sized sails to see which works best.

Rocket balloon

Air makes this balloon rocket along.

You need:
long piece of thread,
straw, long balloon,
sticky tape, peg.

Thread the string through the straw. Then tie it between two chairs.

Blow the balloon up and peg the end to keep the air from coming out. Tape the straw to the balloon.

Tape loosely.

Move the straw to the end of the string and take the peg off the balloon.

See how the balloon flattens as it speeds along.

The trapped air rushes out and makes the balloon move forward.

Windmills

Windmills were once used for grinding corn into flour. The wind turned sails to make machinery work inside.

Sail

Wind winch

This model winch can pull things up and down.

ou need:
thin cardboard,
model dough,
straw, pegs,
thread, 2
cocktail sticks,
buttons, pencil,
tracing paper,
sticky paper.

1. Trace the circle shape below on to cardboard. Cut out the middle. Then cut along the straight lines to make blades.

2. Bend each blade slightly. Then push the circle on to a straw. Hold it in place with model dough.

Trace this shape.

Bend all the blades the same way.

3. Use model dough to stand the pegs up at the edge of a table, so you can fit the straw between them. Push the cocktail sticks through the pegs, into the straw.

Put the pegs upside-down

4. Tie or stick a thread to the straw. Tie a button to the thread.

Blow here.

The thread hangs over the edge of the table.

5. Blow along the straw to make the winch wind up the thread. Put more buttons on to see how much your winch can lift at one time.

13

Moving through air

Some things travel through air better than others. Here you can find out why.

Paper puzzle

Tear two sheets of paper from the same pad. Screw one sheet up into a ball.

Both sheets are the same size.

Hold both pieces at the same height and drop them at the same time.

Can you guess which piece will land first?

Air pushes up on the paper pieces as they drop. The flat one is a bigger shape so more air can push against it. This makes it fall more slowly than the ball.

Pyramid pointer

Fold a square of paper in half from corner to corner. Open it and fold the other corners together.

◄ When you open the paper again you see four triangles.

Pinch one triangle in. ► Push its sides together so you can tape them.

Sides of triangle

Now drop the finished pyramid several times to see which way up it lands.

Try dropping the pyramid point-upward.

The pyramid always lands point first because the pointed end moves faster through the air than the wide end.

Air

Make a parachute

Parachutes are shaped so that lots of air can push against them.

You need: plastic bag scissors, bucket, felt-tipped pen, sticky tape, thread, model dough, very light toy

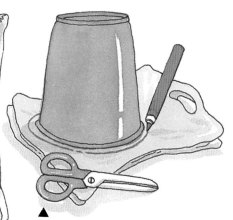

▲

1. Put the bucket on the bag. Draw around it and cut the circle out.

◀ 2. Tape four pieces of long thread to the circle like this.

3. Tie the ends together and push the knot into the model dough. Press the model dough on to the toy.

*Plastic modeling clay

4. Hold the top of the parachute and drop it from a height.

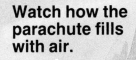

Watch how the parachute fills with air.

Air pushes up against the parachute so the toy falls slowly. Try this with slightly heavier toys. Do they fall any faster?

Go-faster shapes
Fast cars have smooth, pointed shapes. The air flows around these shapes instead of pushing against them. Shapes like this are called streamlined.

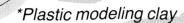

Flying

Planes can fly because of the way air pushes against them.

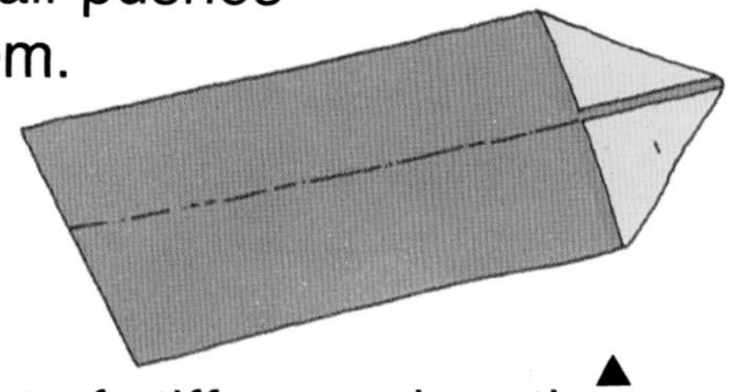

Make a glider

Fold a sheet of stiff paper lengthways. Then open the paper and fold two of the corners inward, as shown above.

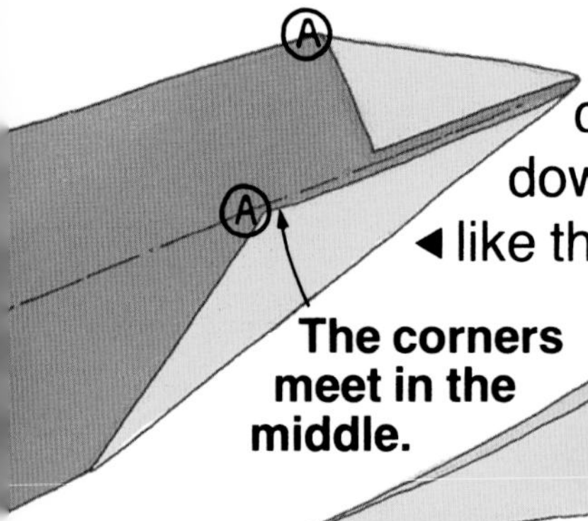

Fold the new corners marked A down to the middle ◄ like this.

The corners meet in the middle.

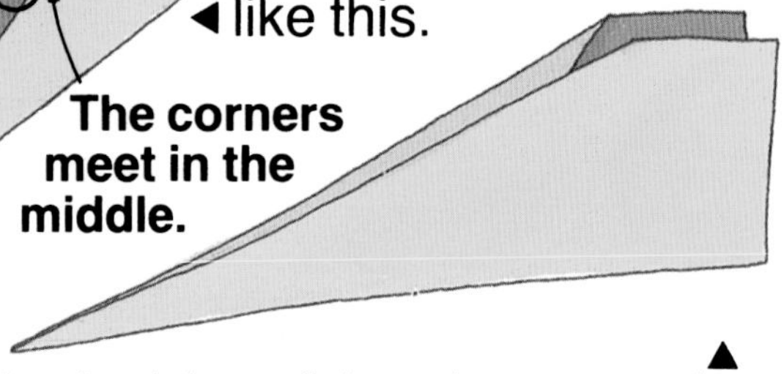

Fold both sides of the plane together with the folded corners inside.

Then fold the top edges down to make a wing on each side.

▼

Fold the wings down one at a time.

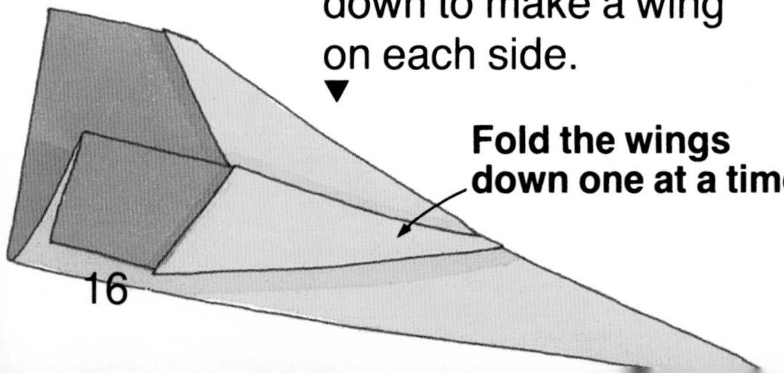

Make a rudder by folding a small square of paper into a triangle.

Fold the corners together.

Glue the rudder between the wings at the back of the plane. Then cut slits to make one flap in the rudder and one on each wing.

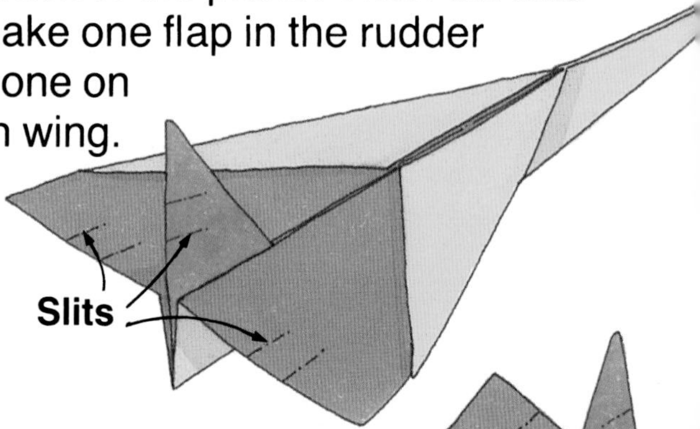

Slits

Flying the glider

Try throwing the glider gently forward.

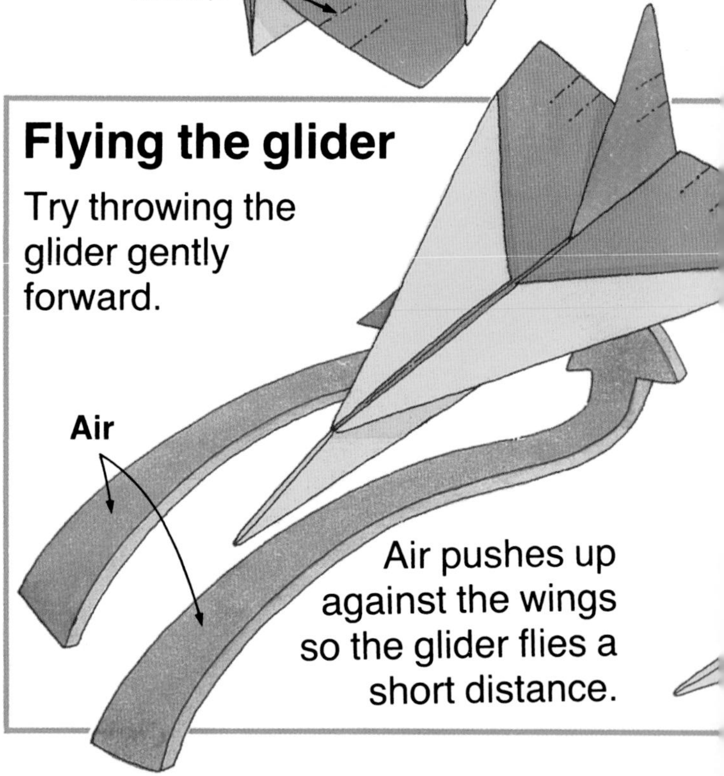

Air

Air pushes up against the wings so the glider flies a short distance.

16

Rising paper

Hold the edge of a sheet of paper just beneath your mouth. Blow across the top of the paper.

← **Blow hard.**

The paper rises because the air beneath pushes harder than the fast-moving air above.

How planes fly

Faster air

Slower air

This shows a slice through the wing.

Planes have wings which are curved on top. When the plane moves, the air travels faster across the curved top.

The slower-moving air beneath pushes harder than the air above. This lifts the heavy plane up so it can fly.

Bend the rudder flap to ▶ the right. How does the plane fly now? What happens if you bend the flap to the left?

Bend this flap.

Bend these wing flaps.

Fly the plane with both wing flaps up and then down. Try again with one ◀ flap up and one down.

The air pushes against the flaps, making the glider turn, climb or dive.

How pilots steer

All planes have flaps on their wings and rudder. The pilot steers the plane by pressing levers which move these flaps.

17

Breathing air

Your body needs air all the time. You get it by breathing in.

Counting breaths

For this experiment, ask a friend to time you with a watch that shows seconds.

Activity	Breaths per 30 secs
Standing still	10
Running	

You could make a chart like this.

Stand still and count the number of breaths you take in 30 seconds. Write this down.

Then run in place. Count your breaths again for 30 seconds. Is there a difference?

Your body uses part of the air you breathe in to help make energy. You need more energy when you run so you breathe faster.

18

Breathing bags

The air is made up of a mixture of gases. One of them is called oxygen. This is the part your body uses.

When you breathe in, you suck air into two spongy bags called lungs. They pass oxygen from the air into your body. You breathe out the rest of the air.

Your lungs are in your chest.

Oxygen travels in your blood.

Cleaning air

Your nose is full of tiny hairs. These trap dust from the air to keep you from breathing it in.

How much can you breathe?

Here is a way to measure how much air your lungs can hold. Get a friend to help you try it.

1. Fill a plastic bottle full of water and push it neck-down into a big bowl of water.

Put your hand over the top until the neck is underwater.

2. Turn the bottle upside-down, keeping the neck underwater. Push a flexible straw into the neck.

Be careful not to squash the straw.

3. Take a deep breath and blow gently down the straw.

The air goes to the top of the bottle.

One person holds the straw in place.

Water in the air

Breathe on a window. Can you see or feel anything on the glass?

Does the glass feel wet?

There is water in the air. When air meets a cold surface, this water appears as tiny drops.

The space at the top of the bottle shows how much air you breathe out. Let your friend try this experiment. See who breathes out the most air.

19

Sound and air

Try these experiments to find out how sound is made and how it travels through the air.

Shaking sound

Stretch an elastic band between your fingers and pluck it to make a sound.

The band vibrates, which means it moves back and forth quickly. Sound is made when something vibrates.

See how the band moves.

How you make sound

Put your fingers on the lump in the middle of your throat and see what you can feel when you sing.

When you make a sound, parts in your throat vibrate. You can feel them shaking.

Sound-catcher

Smooth some newspaper over one end of a cardboard tube and tape it in place.

Sing through the tube and feel the paper at the same time.

The paper must be tight and flat.

Sing here.

Sound vibrations

The sound you make sends vibrations through the air in the tube. These make the paper shake.

Silent space

Out in space there is no noise because there is no air. Sound vibrations cannot travel through empty space.

Bottle music

Blow across the top of an empty bottle. See if you can make a sound.

When you blow across the top, you make the air vibrate inside the bottle. It makes a noise.

Put different amounts of water in the bottle. See if the sound changes.

The water pushes out some of the air.

The more water you put in, the less air there is left in the bottle. Smaller amounts of air vibrate more quickly and this makes a higher sound.

Musical pipes

Lots of musical instruments make sounds because air vibrates inside them. Here is one you can make.

Your breath makes air vibrate inside the straws.

Cut some straws to different lengths. Starting with the shortest, lay them one by one on a piece of sticky tape.

Leave the longest straws till last.

Place another piece of sticky tape on top. Hold the row up and blow across each straw. See which makes the highest sound.

21

Notes for parents and teachers

These notes are intended to help answer questions that arise from the activities on earlier pages.

Air all around (pages 2-3)

Air like other gases, does not have a fixed shape. It spreads out to fill any available space so nothing is really empty. But air cannot escape from the atmosphere as the force of gravity keeps it from floating away from the Earth.

Air that pushes (pages 4-5)

Gases exert pressure in all directions. The pressure is affected by the amount of gas in a given space. When air is pumped into a tire, the valve keeps the air from escaping. As more and more air is pumped into the enclosed space, its pressure increases and it pushes strongly on the tire, keeping it inflated.

The trapped air pushes against the sides of the tire.

Changing size (pages 6-7)

Like most things, air is made up of tiny particles called molecules. When air is heated, its molecules move more quickly and spread out so a given amount of air takes up more space. If the air is contained so it cannot expand, its pressure increases instead.

When air is cooled, its molecules slow down and move nearer to each other. Its pressure then decreases.

Rising air (pages 8-9)

Because air molecules spread out when heated, a certain volume of hot air is lighter than the same volume of cold air. This makes the hot air rise, and float above the cold air.

Wind (pages 10-11)

The wind frequently changes its direction and speed. The faster a wind moves, the more strongly its effects are felt.

Air power (pages 12-13)

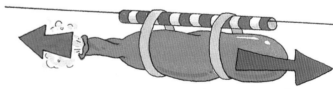

The air inside the rocket balloon is under greater pressure than the air outside. When the peg is taken off, the pressurized air rushes out of the balloon. Newton's third scientific law states that to every action there is an equal and opposite reaction. The balloon obeys this law by moving in the opposite direction to the escaping air.

Moving through air (pages 14-15)

When things move through air, they have to overcome the air pressure rushing against them. This slowing-down effect of the air is called air resistance. Some shapes encounter more air resistance than others.

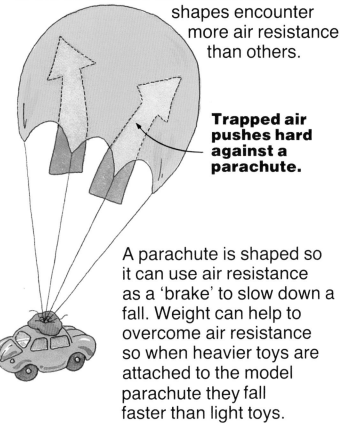

Trapped air pushes hard against a parachute.

A parachute is shaped so it can use air resistance as a 'brake' to slow down a fall. Weight can help to overcome air resistance so when heavier toys are attached to the model parachute they fall faster than light toys.

Flying (pages 16-17)

The fast-flowing air above a plane's wing is at a lower pressure than the slower-moving air beneath. The difference in pressure results in a 'lift' which is strong enough to support the weight of the plane.

Breathing (pages 18-19)

When air is taken into your lungs, some of the oxygen dissolves into your bloodstream. The blood carries oxygen to every cell in your body and takes carbon dioxide gas (a waste-product of the cells) back to the lungs. The carbon dioxide is exhaled together with the parts of the air, such as nitrogen gas, that the body cannot use.

Carbon dioxide goes in.

Oxygen goes out.

Sound (pages 20-21)

Sound is a form of traveling energy produced when an object vibrates. The vibrations travel through the air and make your eardrum begin to vibrate. Your nervous system registers these vibrations as sound.

Tricks with air

Air behaves in many surprising ways. You can use it to make these tricks work.

Magic straw

You can make water stay in a straw for as long as you like.

First, sip some water up into the straw. Take it out of your mouth and put your finger on top.

Keep the straw upright.

The water stays in the straw until you take your finger off. Then air gets in the top of the straw and pushes the water out.

You can stop and start the water whenever you like, just by moving your finger.

Waterproof tissue

You can amaze your friends by keeping a tissue dry underwater.

Stuff the tissue tightly into a glass so it cannot fall out. Turn the glass over and push it into a bowl of water.

Air

Keep the glass straight.

As long as you keep the glass straight the tissue will still be dry when you take the glass out.

This works because the air inside the glass stops the water from getting in. The water can only get in if you tilt the glass so the air escapes.

SCIENCE IN THE KITCHEN

Consultant: Julie Deegan

Contents

Experimenting in the kitchen

Lots of exciting scientific things happen in your kitchen every day. This part of the book explores these things. The first experiments are about cleaning up.

Cleaning birds

Sea-birds can get covered in spilled oil, which water cannot wash off by itself. People use a cleaner like dishwashing liquid to remove the oil.

Helping to mix

Try this experiment to find out how dishwashing liquid helps to make things clean.

1. Smear a little butter on a plate. Hold the plate under the cold tap. Does the water make the plate clean?

Does the water mix with the butter?

2. Add a little dishwashing liquid to the butter and mix it in with your fingers.

3. Hold the plate under the tap again. What happens this time?

Does the water still roll off the butter?

Dishwashing liquid helps water to mix with things better than it can on its own. This is how it helps to make things clean.

Making bubbles

Mix four large spoonfuls of dishwashing liquid into a small glass of water.

Twist a piece of thin wire to make a loop with a handle. Dip the loop right into the mixture. What do you see when you take it out?

Look carefully at the loop.

Blow steadily through the loop, and watch what happens.

Dishwashing liquid can spread out very thin. This is why it can stretch across the loop. It can even stretch around the air you blow out, to make a bubble.

Washing bubbles

Dishwashing liquid stretches around tiny pockets of air trapped in running water. This is how it makes bubbles on the water.

Spreading out

Try this to see how far dishwashing liquid can spread out.

Sprinkle talcum powder on a bowl of water. Add a drop of dishwashing liquid. Watch what happens.

The dishwashing liquid pushes the talcum powder away as it spreads out over the surface of the water.

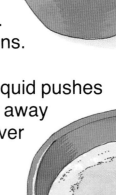

27

Soaked through

What things do you use to mop up spills? They need to be good at soaking up water.

Dish-cloth

Tissue

Tracing paper

Soaking up

Collect different things, to see which soaks up water best. Here are some things you could try.

Try to find pieces about the same size.

Cotton

Pour a teaspoon of water onto a saucer. To test each thing, put it on the water. Count to five, then take it away. Does it soak up all the water?

Coffee filter paper

Plastic

Use a new spoonful of water for each test.

Some things leave water behind. Dry the saucer before you test each thing.

Feeling the difference

Feel a dry piece of each thing you tested. The things that soak up water feel rougher than the things that don't, because they are full of tiny holes. The holes let the water in.

Sponges

Bath sponges soak up water very well. You can see the holes that let the water in.

28

Marble test

Try this strength test on three or four things that soak up water. Secure each one over an empty plastic pot with a rubber band. Put a marble on top.

Drop a spoonful of water on each marble, and watch what happens.

Do the marbles move?

Which marble sinks down the least?

Some things get weak when they are wet and let the marble drop. Things that mop up well need to stay strong.

Soaking colors

See what happens when water soaks through colors from felt-tip pens.

Put a big color dot near one end of each paper strip.

Pour some water into the saucer. Put the colored end of each strip in the water. Watch what happens.

You need: strips of coffee filter paper, felt-tip pens (dark colors are best), saucer.

Is the color the same all the way up?

Most colors are made up of other colors. They separate out as water soaks through them.

29

Disappearing water

Have you ever wondered what happens to the water in wet things when they dry?

Drying out

Soak two dishcloths in water and wring them out so they are just damp.

Spread one cloth on a plate. Put the other in a plastic bag and tape it shut. Leave them in a warm place. Which cloth do you think will dry first?

Feel the cloths the next day. Which one is driest?

Wet things dry out because tiny water drops escape from them into the air. This is called evaporation.

The cloth in the bag stays wet, because the water cannot reach the air.

Getting water back

Look at the bathroom mirror when you have had a bath.

What can you see? Touch the glass. Is it wet?

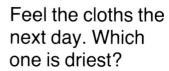

Water evaporates from your bath. When the tiny drops in the air hit something cool, like the mirror, they join up to make drops that you can see.

Salty water test

Stir two teaspoons of salt into a small bowl of warm water. Taste a tiny bit of the water to find out how salty it is.*

Cover the bowl with clear plastic and leave it in a warm place.

Look at it after an hour. What do you see on the inside of the plastic?

This water has evaporated from the bowl.

Taste the water on the plastic.* Is it salty?

When water evaporates, anything mixed in it is left behind.

Never taste things unless an adult says they are safe to eat.

Rainbow sugar

You can use evaporation to make colored sugar crystals to eat.

You need:
2 spoons of sugar,
10 spoons of water,
food color,
foil dishes or
saucers covered
with foil.

Stir the sugar into the water until it disappears.

Pour two spoonfuls onto each foil dish.

Add a different food color to each dish. Leave the dishes in a warm place for three days.

The water evaporates and leaves behind colored sugar crystals. You can break them up and mix them to make rainbow sugar.

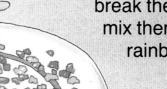

31

Wet and dry

Most food has water in it. Some food is dried to take the water out.

Pop the lid

Find a small plastic pot with a lid. Fill it with dried peas, and pour in cold water up to the top.

Stand the pot on a saucer, and put on the lid.

Look at the pot the next day. What has happened? Take out the peas. How much water is left?

Each pea has gotten much bigger.

The peas get big enough to push the lid off the pot because they take in water. Dry food can soak up lots of water.*

Knock down the tower

Make a tower of four sugar lumps on a plate. Add a little food coloring to some water. Pour it onto the plate and watch what happens.

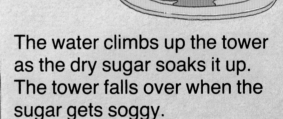

Watch the bottom of the tower.

The water climbs up the tower as the dry sugar soaks it up. The tower falls over when the sugar gets soggy.

The color helps you see how high the water climbs.

The peas must be soaked overnight and cooked to make them good to eat.

Drying things out

Sprinkle sugar on a slice of cucumber. Leave it for ten minutes. Has anything changed?

Can you see water on the cucumber?

Sugar soaks up water so well that it can draw water out of cucumber.

Drying to keep

Try this experiment to find out why food is dried.

Cut a slice of bread in half. Leave one piece in a warm, sunny place until it feels dry. Sprinkle water on the other piece.

Put each piece in a clear plastic bag. Tape the bags loosely shut. Label them "wet" and "dry". **Cellophane tape**

Leave the bags in a warm place. Look at them after four days to see if any mold has grown. Which piece is the most moldy?*

Keep the bags closed all the time.

Mold

Mold grows best on wet food. Food is dried so that mold does not grow on it so quickly. This means it can keep for a long time.

Adventure food

Explorers take dried food with them, because it keeps for a long time and it is light to carry.

* Throw the bags away when you have finished the experiment.

33

Juice

Every sort of fruit has juice in it. Juice is mostly made up of water.*

Looking at juice

Look at an orange segment. Does it feel wet? Can you see the juice inside it?

Orange segment

Hold the segment over a plate and squeeze it very hard. Can you feel the juice now?

Is the juice the same color as the orange? Does it taste the same?

Is the segment in your hand as big as before?

Juice takes up most of the space in fruit. It has most of the color and flavor in it.

Water in everything

Every living thing, including you, has water in it. Your body is about two-thirds water.

Getting juice out

See how easy it is to get juice out of different sorts of fruit. Here are some you could try.

Kiwi fruit

Raspberry

Blackberry

Pear

Apple

Lemon segment

It may help if you squash the fruit with a spoon.

Juice is held in tiny bags called cells. You have to break the cells to get it out. The cells in some sorts of fruit are harder to break than others.

An orange's cells are big enough to see, and easy to break.

34   * These experiments are messy, so wear old clothes to do them.

Colorful juice

You can do this experiment with brightly colored juice, like raspberry or blackberry juice. You also need an old white cotton handkerchief.

Make a simple pattern on the handkerchief with colorful juice. Leave it to dry.

Next day, wash the handkerchief under the tap. Can you still see any color?

The color in juice can stain material. It is very hard to wash off.

Invisible ink

Draw a picture on white paper with lemon juice. The picture is hard to see when it is dry.

Keep dipping your finger in the juice.

Ask an adult to iron your invisible picture with a hot iron. The picture appears almost instantly, because the heat from the iron turns the lemon juice brown.

Picture after ironing

Dyes

People can use juice from fruit, flowers, or bark to make cloth interesting colors. Juice colors are called natural dyes.

35

Taste tests

The way food tastes helps you decide whether you like eating it.*

Tongue test

You taste things with your tongue. It tells you whether things are sweet, like sugar, or bitter, like coffee.

Make sure your hands are clean for this test.

Dip a finger in powdered sugar. Dab it on the back of your tongue, then one side, then tip. Where does it taste sweet?

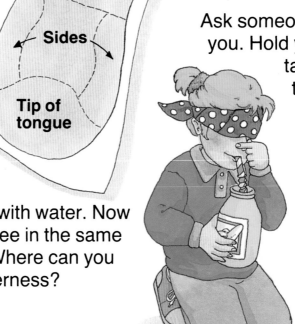

Back of tongue

← **Sides** →

Tip of tongue

Rinse your mouth with water. Now test cold black coffee in the same three places. Where can you taste the bitterness?

Different parts of your tongue notice sweet tastes and bitter ones.

Smelling taste

Why doesn't food taste as good when you have a cold? Try this to find out.

You need a blindfold and two drinks with straws in them. You could try strawberry and banana milkshakes.

Ask someone to blindfold you. Hold your nose and taste one drink, then the other. Can you tell which is which?

Your tongue can only tell you that both the drinks taste sweet. It cannot tell them apart.

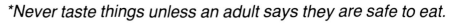

Never taste things unless an adult says they are safe to eat.

Try the test again, but don't hold your nose. Can you taste the difference now?

Your nose notices different flavors that your tongue cannot taste.

You cannot tell flavors apart when you have a cold because your nose is blocked.

Treading on taste

Flies taste food with their feet. They walk all over food to find out if it is good to eat.

Funny colors

Colors help you to guess how food will taste before you eat it. See what happens if you change the color of food.

Use food coloring to make food funny colors. You could give people green scrambled eggs, purple mashed potato and blue milk.

Watch their faces as they taste the food. Do they want to eat it?

If food is a funny color, you think it will taste horrible. This helps to keep you safe, because food sometimes changes color when it goes bad.

37

Sour things

Acids are chemicals that can be dangerous. But lemons and other foods have safe, weak acids in them. They tend to taste sour.*

Tasting sourness

Taste different sorts of food and drink to see which might be acid. Here are some things you could try. Can you guess which ones will taste sour?

Milk
Vinegar
Soft drink
Water
Orange
Salt
Yogurt
Sugar
Grapefruit

Try making a chart to show which things taste sour.

taste sour
vinegar
soft drink

Red cabbage test

You can make red cabbage water to help you test for acid food.

You need:
half a red cabbage,
hot water,
saucepan,
sieve, clean jug,
jars or glasses.

Tear the red cabbage leaves into little pieces. Put them in the saucepan.

Ask an adult to pour boiling water into the saucepan. Let it cool for half an hour.

Pour the cabbage water through a sieve into a jug.

You don't need the cabbage bits.

Look at the cabbage water to see what color it is. Pour some into each jar.

Never taste things unless an adult says they are safe to eat.

Add some lemon juice to one jar. Does anything change?

Red cabbage water changes color from purple to pink when you add acid to it. Things that are not acid leave the cabbage water purple or turn it green.

Try adding the other things that taste sour to jars of red cabbage water. Do they all turn it pink?

Now try adding the things which do not taste sour. Are any of them acid?

Some acid things, like soft drinks, don't taste sour because there is lots of sugar in them.

Don't drink the cola. Throw it away.

Cola clean

Drop a dirty copper coin into a glass of cola.

Take out the coin the next day. Has it changed?

Is the coin still dirty?

The acid in cola is strong enough to eat away the dirt on the coin.*

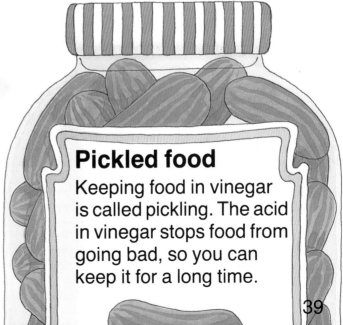

Pickled food

Keeping food in vinegar is called pickling. The acid in vinegar stops food from going bad, so you can keep it for a long time.

39

Fizz

Have you noticed tiny bubbles in soft drinks? Try these experiments to find out more about these bubbles.

Going up

Pour some clear soft drink into a big jar. Can you see the bubbles? They are full of gas.

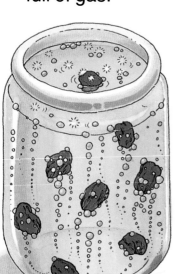

Drop in some raisins and watch what happens.

Bubbles stick to the raisins. The gas in them is so light that they can carry the raisins to the top of the drink.

The bubbles burst at the top. The light gas escapes, so the raisins sink. More bubbles stick to them at the bottom, and they go up again.

Making a fizz

This experiment uses bicarbonate of soda. It is used in baking, and you can buy it at a supermarket.

Put a spoonful of vinegar in a glass. Sprinkle in a spoonful of bicarbonate of soda. Watch what happens.

When you mix an acid*, like vinegar, with bicarbonate of soda, gas fizzes out.

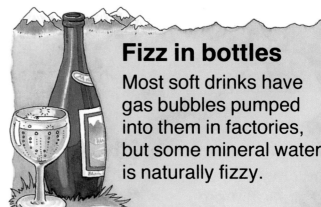

Fizz in bottles

Most soft drinks have gas bubbles pumped into them in factories, but some mineral water is naturally fizzy.

* You can find out more about acids on pages 38-39.

Fizz in your mouth

You can make a sweet treat that fizzes with citric acid, which you can buy at a pharmacy or wine-making shop.

You need:
2 spoons of citric acid crystals,
1 spoon of bicarbonate of soda,
8 spoons of powdered sugar, bowl.

Mix up the ingredients in a bowl. It doesn't fizz until you put a little dab in your mouth. Then you can feel the gas escaping.

The acid and bicarbonate of soda can only fizz together when they get wet. The wetness in your mouth makes the mixture fizz.

Test this by dropping water on a spoonful of the mixture.

Heat bubbles

Carefully pour some very hot tap water into a clear heat-proof bowl. Add a spoonful of bicarbonate of soda.

You will need to look very closely to see the tiny bubbles.

Bicarbonate can fizz without acid when it gets very hot.

Cake bubbles

The holes in a piece of cake are bubbles made by bicarbonate of soda in the cake mixture.

The bicarbonate makes the bubbles when the mixture gets hot in the oven. This makes the cake rise.

41

Dough

When you mix flour with oil and water, you make it into something completely different, called dough. Here you can find out more about dough.

Craft dough (salt based)

You need:
10 heaped tablespoons plain flour,
1 teaspoon salt,
4 teaspoons oil,
8 tablespoons warm water,
bowl.

Mix the flour and salt in a bowl. Pour in the oil. Add the water bit by bit, mixing it in with your other hand.

Stop adding water if the dough gets sticky.

Adding heat

You can make models from craft dough. If you want to keep them, ask an adult to help you bake them.*

The heat in the oven turns the dough hard.

Stretch and squash the dough until it all holds together.

Does it feel like flour now? How many differences can you find? You could write them on a chart.

Whatever you do, you cannot turn dough back into flour.

flour	dough
dry powdery	wet squashy

Dough for bread

If you add yeast to flour, water and oil, you can make dough for bread.

You need:
flour, oil,
warm water and salt
as for craft dough,
3 teaspoons of
dried yeast,
1 teaspoon sugar,
a glass, bowl,
baking tray,
plastic bag.

Make sure your hands are clean.

Mix the flour and salt. Pour in the oil and the yeast mixture. Slowly add the rest of the water. Mix and squash the dough.

Shape the dough into six rolls. Put them on a baking tray.

Mix the yeast and sugar in the glass. Stir in half the warm water.

Cover the tray with a plastic bag. Put it in a warm place. Look at the rolls after 20 minutes. Are they still the same size?

Leave it for 15 minutes. Watch what happens.

Gas bubbles

The rolls get bigger because the yeast makes bubbles in the dough.

Yeast is a living thing. When it has sugar, water and warmth, it grows and makes bubbles of gas.

Take off the plastic bag, and ask an adult to cook the rolls.*

When the rolls have cooled, break one open and look inside.

The bubbles of gas have left holes in the rolls.

See page 47 for cooking times and temperatures.

Freezing and melting

Water changes into ice when it gets very cold. Can you guess what happens to other things?

Frozen food

Food can be kept frozen for months. When it is warmed up again, it is still good to eat.

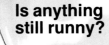

Making things cold

Put a spoonful or a small lump of different things in the sections of an ice-cube tray. Put it in the freezer.*

You could try: tomato ketchup, fruit juice, syrup, oil, milk, cheese, butter, chocolate.

Take the things out after two hours. Tip them onto a tray. Has anything changed?

Feel things to find out how hard they are.

Most things get hard, like ice, when they get cold enough. This is called freezing.

Ice to eat

An ice pop is like a frozen drink on a stick. The warmth in your mouth makes the pop melt.

Some things, like oil, need to be very cold indeed before they freeze. Even the freezer may not be cold enough to make them go hard.

Is anything still runny?

You could use the ice-making compartment of a refrigerator.

Warming up

Frozen things soften when they warm up. Some things get runny when you take them out of the freezer. This is called melting. Try this to see if ice always melts at the same speed.

You need:
2 mugs,
2 ice-cubes,
cotton,
plastic wrap.

Wrap one mug in cotton. Put an ice-cube in each mug and cover them both with plastic wrap.

Leave the mugs in a warm room. Which ice-cube do you think will melt first?

Look at the mugs every ten minutes to see if you are right.

Oven gloves

Oven gloves help to keep heat out. People wear them to protect their hands from hot things.

The ice-cube in the unwrapped mug melts first because warmth from the room gets in quickly. The other ice-cube stays frozen longer because warmth cannot get through cotton so quickly.

45

Notes for parents and teachers

These notes are intended to help answer questions that arise from the activities on earlier pages.

Experimenting in the kitchen (pages 26-27)

Like most things, water and dishwashing liquid (detergent) are made up of molecules. Detergent molecules are long, and only one end of them attracts water molecules. The other end attracts other things, like butter and dirt. This is how detergent makes a link between water and things which do not dissolve in water.

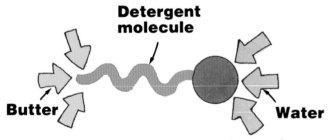

Detergent spreads out over the surface of water because the detergent molecules line up, each with one end away from the water.

Soaked through (pages 28-29)

Water molecules attract each other very strongly, so when a little water moves into a gap in a fabric, its molecules pull in more water. This helps water to soak into things.

Disappearing water (pages 30-31)

When water evaporates, its molecules move into the air. They spread apart, forming invisible water vapor. When water vapor touches a cool surface, the molecules join together again to make small water drops that you can see. This is called condensation.

Wet and dry (pages 32-33)

Mold and bacteria are living things that need water to survive. This is why drying food tends to prevent them from growing, and so preserve the food.

Bacteria that need air to live are less dangerous than the sort that don't need air. The bags of bread must only be sealed loosely so air can get inside, to encourage the safer sort of bacteria to grow. You should still take care, and keep the bags closed even when you are throwing them away.

Taste tests (pages 36-37)

Different areas of your tongue have taste buds that detect different basic tastes, and send messages to your brain about them. There are four basic tastes – sweet, bitter, sour (like lemon juice), and salty. You can test sour and salty tastes in the same way as sweetness and bitterness. This tongue map shows the areas where each taste can be detected.

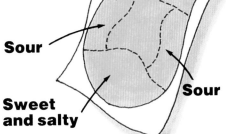

Bitter

Sour

Sweet and salty

Sour

Sour things (pages 38-39)

Red cabbage water is an indicator. This means that it changes color when it is mixed with acids or other chemicals called alkalis. Alkalis turn it greeny-blue. Bicarbonate of soda is a safe alkali that you can test, but most alkalis in the kitchen are cleaning substances and may not be safe to handle.

Red cabbage water mixed with bicarbonate of soda

If you mix acid and alkali in the right proportions, they neutralize each other, and have no effect on cabbage water.

Neutral things leave red cabbage water purple.

Dough (pages 42-43)

Cooking instructions – bake craft dough models at 180°C, 350°F, Gas mark 4 for 30 minutes. They will only keep for a long time if they are really dried out. Bake rolls at 230°C, 450°F, Gas mark 7 for 15 minutes.

Yeast is a fungus. In dried form, it is dormant, but providing it with warmth, water and food (sugar) reactiviates it. It produces carbon dioxide bubbles which become holes in the bread. The yeast is killed by the intense heat in the oven so the bread stops rising.

Freezing and melting (pages 44-45)

Cotton doesn't let heat through quickly because it contains trapped air, which does not conduct heat well. Other spongy materials also make good insulators.

Trapped air between the cotton fibers

Extraordinary eggs

Here are a couple of tricks you can do with eggs.

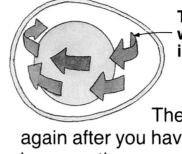

This shows what happens inside the egg.

Spin the egg

This is a clever way to tell a raw egg from a hard-boiled one without breaking them.

Spin each egg on a plate.

Stop them with your hand, and let go right away.

The fresh egg spins again after you have stopped it because the runny yolk and white keep spinning inside the shell.

The insides of the hard-boiled egg cannot spin, so once you have stopped it, it stays still.

You can crack the eggs to prove you are right.

Egg shell challenge

Ask a friend to hold an egg lengthwise between her palms. Bet that she cannot squeeze the egg hard enough like this to break it.

Unless the egg is cracked before you start, your friend will not be able to break it. An egg's shape is so strong that it is very hard to squash.

SCIENCE WITH
PLANTS

Consultant: Dr. Margaret Rostron

Contents

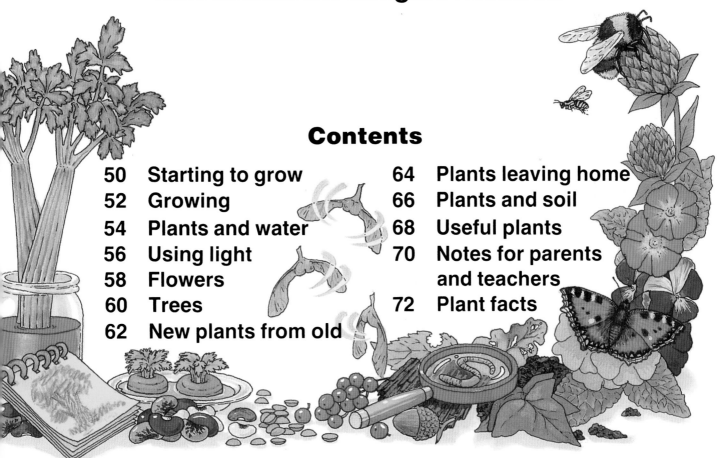

Starting to grow

Plants grow almost everywhere. This book has lots of experiments and activities to help you find out how plants live and grow.

Look around for useful things to help you grow plants, such as jars and other containers. You may need to buy some things such as flower pots and potting compost.*

Writing it down

Try keeping a nature diary to make notes and drawings about plants and your experiments. Always write the date, so you can remember when things happened and how long they took.

Looking at seeds

Plants make seeds so new plants can grow. Can you find any seeds like these in your kitchen at home?

Lentils

Rice

Dried beans

Beans are the seeds of bean plants. Look closely at a dried bean. Can you break it with your fingers?

A hard case protects the bean.

A scar shows where the bean was attached to its plant.

Soak a bean in water overnight to make it soft. Split it open carefully. What can you see inside?

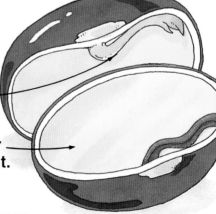

Here is a tiny baby plant, ready to grow.

This part is a food store for the baby plant.

*You can buy these at a garden centre.

Growing beans

Line two jars with paper towels and add a little water. Put some dried kidney beans next to the glass, half-way up each jar. Keep them indoors.

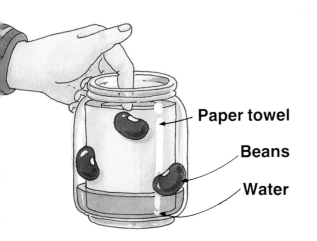

Paper towel

Beans

Water

Wait for a week. What can you see?

This is called a shoot.

This is called a root.

The beans have germinated. This means they have sprouted shoots and roots and the baby plants are ready to start growing.

Different seeds

Seeds come in different shapes and sizes. They are often inside a cover like a fruit, a shell or a pod. Here are some you might find at home.

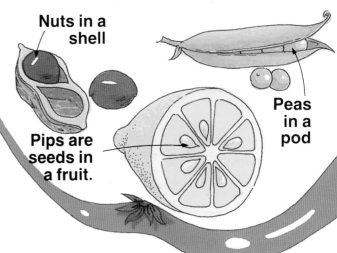

Nuts in a shell

Pips are seeds in a fruit.

Peas in a pod

Up and down

Leave one jar on its side for a few days. What happens to the way the shoots and roots grow?

Shoots always grow up towards sunlight and roots always grow down towards the ground and water.

The shoot bends up again.

The root bends down again.

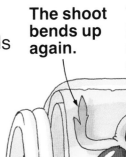

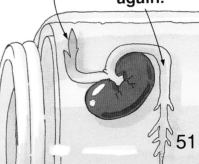

51

Growing

After a seed has germinated, the young plant starts to grow. Look at the beans you germinated before (see page 51). What do you notice as they grow?

The shoots have grown leaves.

The first two leaves are very small. They are called seed leaves.

The seed cases have withered away. They are not needed anymore.

More roots have begun to grow.

How to plant beans

First fill some plastic flower pots with damp potting compost. Poke a hole in the compost with a pencil, deep enough for a seedling's roots.

Leave a dish under each pot to catch water.

Carefully take the paper towel out of the jars. Lift off the seedlings and plant one in each pot.

Push the compost down firmly around each seedling to keep it upright. Leave enough space at the top of the pot for water.

As each bean grows, its roots spread out into the compost. They take up water and hold the plant steady.

52

Healthy growing

What things do you think plants need to help them grow? Try this experiment with your potted beans to see if you are right.

Put labels on three of the pots. Put pot 1 near a window. Water it every three days.

Put pot 2 near a window but do not water it.

Put pot 3 in a dark cupboard. Water it every three days.

After three weeks see which plant has grown best.

Pot 1 should grow best because it has soil, light and water. Plants need all these things to stay healthy.

Speedy grower

Bamboo is an enormous kind of grass that grows very fast in hot countries. In wet years it can grow one metre (39 inches) in a day.

Giant pandas eat bamboo.

How fast?

How fast do your bean plants grow? Hold some cardboard beside each one and measure its height each day.

You can tie a tall plant to a stick to keep it straight.

How high is each plant after a month? Keep notes in your nature diary.

53

Plants and water

Water gets into a plant from the ground through the roots. What do you think happens to it next?

Climbing up the stem

Put a stick of celery into a jar of water. Add a few drops of blue ink.

Leave the jar near a window for four hours. What happens to the leaves?

The leaves are full of blue inky water. Plants suck water up through the stem into the leaves. They need water to grow and keep healthy.

Water getting out

Cover a potted plant with a clear plastic bag, and tie it around the stem. Stand it in a sunny place. Look at the bag after four hours and rub it with your fingers.

Can you see tiny water droplets?

Plants do not use all the water they take up. They get rid of extra water through tiny holes in their leaves. The bag traps the droplets so you can see them.

Cut a slice from the stem. What can you see?

Tiny blue dots show the tubes that carry water up the stem.

Never put plastic bags near your face or mouth.

Make a bottle garden

You can make a garden that never needs watering. Find a large bottle or jar with a lid. Lay it on its side and fill it with layers like this.

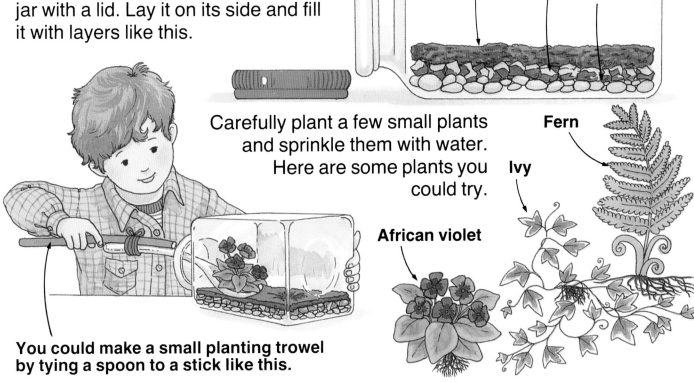

Damp potting compost
Charcoal*
Pebbles

Carefully plant a few small plants and sprinkle them with water. Here are some plants you could try.

Fern

Ivy

African violet

You could make a small planting trowel by tying a spoon to a stick like this.

Put the lid on the bottle and leave it in a warm, light place. The plants should keep on growing healthily.

The plants get water through their roots and lose it through their leaves. It is trapped inside the bottle and trickles down so the plants can use it again and again.

You can get this from a garden centre. 55

Using light

Plants need light to live. These experiments will help you to find out why.

Looking for light

Leave a potted plant in a room with one window. Put it a little way from the window and water it as usual.

What do you notice about the way the plant grows?

Which side do the leaves grow on?

The plant leans towards the light. If you turn the pot around, the plant soon grows back to face the window again. Plants always grow towards light.

56

In the dark

Cover one leaf of a growing plant with foil so that it gets no light.

Take the foil off after a week. What do you notice?

Without light the leaf turns yellow. The other leaves are still green.

Making food

Plants use energy from sunlight to make food. Leaves have special green stuff called chlorophyll, that traps the sun's energy. Without light, leaves cannot make food. They turn yellow and the plant dies.

Looking at leaves

What things do you notice when you look at a leaf?

Chlorophyll makes leaves green.

The stalk holds the leaf out towards the light.

Underside of leaf

These lines are called veins.

Can you feel veins with your fingers? Water moves along them to all parts of a leaf. Veins also take food from the leaf to the rest of the plant.

Leaf shapes

Have you noticed how the leaves on a plant are usually the same shape?

Every plant has different leaves. A leaf's shape can tell you which kind of plant it comes from.

Leaf prints

Collect as many different kinds of leaves as you can.

Put the leaves on some cardboard, and lay a piece of paper over them.

Rub over the paper with a wax crayon or soft pencil to make the shape of the leaf appear.

Always rub in the same direction.

Try using different colors.

Label each leaf so that you know which plant it comes from.

Flowers

Flowers are the parts of plants that make seeds. They come in many shapes, sizes and colours.

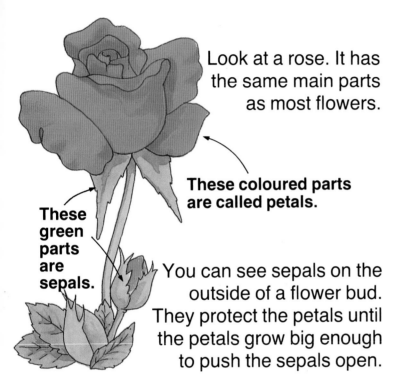

Look at a rose. It has the same main parts as most flowers.

These coloured parts are called petals.

These green parts are sepals.

You can see sepals on the outside of a flower bud. They protect the petals until the petals grow big enough to push the sepals open.

Carefully pull the petals off the rose. How many are there? What shape are they? Can you smell them?

Petals have bright colours and sweet smells to attract insects to the plant.

Shapes and colours

Each kind of flower has different petals, with their own shape, colour and smell. Here are some you might know.

A daffodil's petals are joined together to make a trumpet.➞

A tulip's sepals are the same colour as the petals inside.

An iris's petals have different colours and shapes.

Making seeds

What can you see inside a rose?

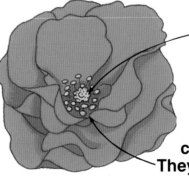

This group of yellow parts right in the middle is called a pistil.

These are called stamens. They grow around the pistil.

The stamens and pistil make seeds for new plants.

Powder

Look at the stamens through a magnifying glass. Gently touch the tips.

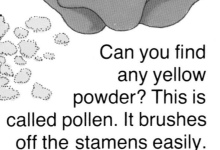

Can you find any yellow powder? This is called pollen. It brushes off the stamens easily.

Sometimes pollen from one flower reaches the pistils of another of the same kind. Then the plant starts to make seeds. This is called pollination.

Smelly flower

The Stapelia flower looks and smells like rotting meat. This attracts flies to it. Pollen sticks to the flies so they carry it from one flower to another.

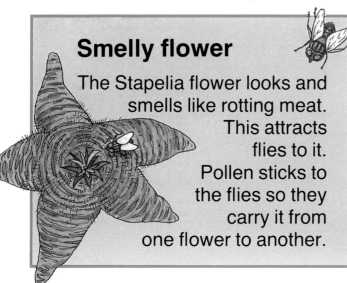

Helpful insects

Look for insects on flowers outside during summer. How many kinds can you see?

Insects come to drink a sweet juice made inside a flower. This is called nectar.

Watch a butterfly on a flower. You can see it drinking nectar with its long tongue.

Tongue

Some pollen sticks to insects. They carry it from one flower to another. This is how most flowers are pollinated.

Lots of pollen sticks to a bee's furry body.

Trees

Trees can grow bigger than any other plants. Look at trees near your home. How tall are they? Are any taller than a house?

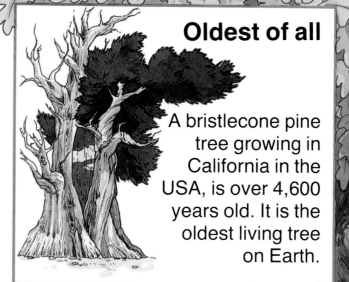

Oldest of all

A bristlecone pine tree growing in California in the USA, is over 4,600 years old. It is the oldest living tree on Earth.

Growing old

Look at the top of a tree stump. What can you see?
There are lots of rings in the wood. Trees make one ring every year. So the number of rings tells you how old the tree is.

The middle rings are the oldest.

This ring was made two years ago.

Stealing the light

Stand under a big tree in summer and look up.* Can you see the sky?

The leaves make food for the tree.

A big tree needs to make lots of food, so it has many leaves. They spread out to catch as much light as possible. This is why you can't see much sky.

*Ask an adult before you go out on your own.

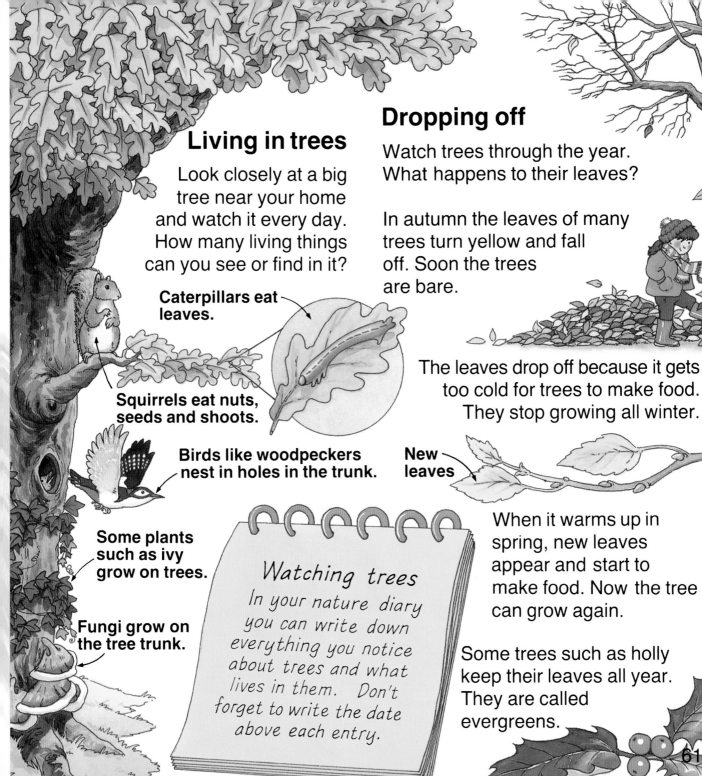

Living in trees

Look closely at a big tree near your home and watch it every day. How many living things can you see or find in it?

Caterpillars eat leaves.

Squirrels eat nuts, seeds and shoots.

Birds like woodpeckers nest in holes in the trunk.

Some plants such as ivy grow on trees.

Fungi grow on the tree trunk.

Watching trees

In your nature diary you can write down everything you notice about trees and what lives in them. Don't forget to write the date above each entry.

Dropping off

Watch trees through the year. What happens to their leaves?

In autumn the leaves of many trees turn yellow and fall off. Soon the trees are bare.

The leaves drop off because it gets too cold for trees to make food. They stop growing all winter.

New leaves

When it warms up in spring, new leaves appear and start to make food. Now the tree can grow again.

Some trees such as holly keep their leaves all year. They are called evergreens.

61

Plants leaving home

If plants grow crowded together, they do not get enough light, soil or water. Plants have lots of different ways to help their seeds spread out into new places.

Getting a lift

After a walk outdoors, carefully scrape the mud off your shoes.*

Put the mud into a wet plastic bag.

Close it and leave it in a warm place. What happens after a week or so?

Can you see shoots starting to grow? Plants have germinated from tiny seeds in the mud. You have helped to spread the plants by carrying their seeds on your shoes.

Clinging on

After your walk look closely at your clothes. Sometimes you can find little round things called burrs stuck there. These have seeds inside.

Look at one burr closely under a magnifying glass. What can you see?

Burr **Tiny hooks**

Burrs have tiny hooks that cling to things like animals' fur or your clothes. In this way the seeds inside are carried away to grow in new places.

Burrs come from plants like this.

Burrs stick to fur.

*Always wear rubber or gardening gloves when handling soil.

Blowing in the wind

Pick the head off a dandelion after the flower has died. What happens when you blow it?

Dandelion seeds are carried by lots of tiny, fluffy parachutes.

The parachutes are so light that the wind can carry them away. How far can you blow them?

Many plants use the wind to scatter their seeds. Look at the seeds of sycamore or maple trees. They are shaped like wings. What happens if you hold one up high and drop it?

The seeds spin like tiny helicopters.

This makes them fall slowly, so breezes have time to blow them away from the tree.

Ask a friend to drop some sycamore seeds. Fan them with a magazine as they fall. How far do they blow?

Looking tasty

Many plants have bright-coloured berries. In winter, berries are eaten by birds like thrushes. They scatter the seeds in their droppings, so the plants are spread to new areas.

Can you find any other seeds that travel by wind? Which ones can you blow the furthest?

Ash seed

Elm seed

65

Plants and soil

Most plants grow in soil. Their roots spread out to keep the plant steady and to find water. These experiments will help you find out more about soil.

Tiny pieces of plants float on top.

This black layer is made of rotted plants. It is called humus.

Heavy stones, sand and clay sink down to the bottom.

Clay

Sand

Stones

Inside soil

What do you think soil is made of? Put a scoop of soil* into a jar with a lid. Add two scoops of water. Put on the lid and give it a good shake. Shake it up again after two hours.

You could use a yogurt pot as a scoop.

Let the jar stand. What can you see one day later?

The soil falls into separate layers. Some soils are mostly clay. Others are more sandy. Different plants prefer different kinds of soil. What is your soil like?

Rotting down

Look at the ground under trees in a wood. What do you notice?

The woodland floor is covered in a layer of dead and rotting leaves called leaf litter.

Close up

Collect some leaf litter in a plastic bag. Shake it out onto paper at home and search through it carefully to see what you can find.*

Humus

Berries

Twigs

Bark

Leaves

Leaf litter is made from bits of plants that gradually break down into compost. The compost rots down into a layer of humus under the leaves.

Acorn

Humus helps to hold water in the soil. Plants take up ingredients with the water called minerals, which help them grow. When plants die, minerals return to the soil and help feed more living plants.

*Remember to wear gloves when handling soil.

Crawling with life

Look more closely at your leaf litter. Can you spot any animals like these?

A magnifying glass helps you to see better.

Centipede

Earthworm

Spider

Soil mite

You can lift them up gently with a paint brush for a closer look. Afterwards put them back where you found them.

Leaf litter is full of living things. They help to break it down by eating it and passing it through their bodies. When they die, their bodies also rot down into humus.

Plant Facts

Here you can find out some amazing facts about different plants.

Giant plants

★ One of the longest plants grows under the sea. The Pacific Kelp is a giant seaweed that can grow to 60m (196ft) long.

★ The Rafflesia is the world's biggest flower. It lives in rainforests in Indonesia, and can grow to nearly 1m (39in) across.

★ Some gardeners can grow enormous fruit. The biggest ever water melon was grown in Arkansas in the USA. It weighed 90kg (200lb). That's heavier than most men.

Ancient plants

Scientists have found fossils that show that Maidenhair Trees lived on Earth over 200 million years ago. Today very similar plants still grow in China.

Slow grower

The Century Plant in America grows very slowly. It only sprouts two to three leaves every year and takes 100 years to flower.

Killer plant

Not all plants make all their food from light. Some, like the Venus Fly Trap, have special leaves that can catch insects for the plant to eat.

If a fly lands on a Venus Fly Trap, the leaves snap shut and trap it.

Index

First published in 1992 by Usborne Publishing Ltd, Usborne House, 83-85 Saffron Hill, London EC1N 8RT, England. www.usborne.com